W9-BXU-355

A Note to Parents and Teachers

DK READERS is a compelling programme for beginning readers, designed in conjunction with literacy experts, including Maureen Fernandes, B.Ed (Hons). Maureen has spent many years teaching literacy, both in the classroom and as a consultant in schools.

Beautiful illustrations and superb full-colour photographs combine with engaging, easy-to-read stories to offer a fresh approach to each subject in the series.

Each DK READER is guaranteed to capture a child's interest while developing his or her reading skills, general knowledge and love of reading.

The five levels of DK READERS are aimed at different reading abilities, enabling you to choose the books that are exactly right for your child:

Pre-level 1: Learning to read

Level 1: Beginning to read

Level 2: Beginning to read alone

Level 3: Reading alone

Level 4: Proficient readers

The "normal" age at which a child begins to read can be anywhere from three to eight years old. Adult participation through the lower levels is very helpful for providing encouragement, discussing storylines and sounding out unfamiliar words.

No matter which level you select, you can be sure that you are helping your child learn to read, then read to learn!

LONDON, NEW YORK, MUNICH,
MELBOURNE, AND DELHI

Designer Hanna Ländin
Project Editor Amy Junor
Brand Manager Lisa Lanzarini
Publishing Manager Simon Beecroft
Category Publisher Alex Allan
Production Editor Sean Daly
Print Production Nick Seston

Reading Consultant
Linda Gambrell

First published in the United States in 2008
by DK Publishing
375 Hudson Street
New York, New York 10014

08 09 10 11 10 9 8 7 6 5 4 3 2 1
DD397 – 11/07

DK books are available at special discounts when purchased in
bulk for sales promotions, premiums, fund-raising, or educational use.
For details, contact:
DK Publishing Special Markets, 375 Hudson Street, New York, New
York 10014
SpecialSales@dk.com

ISBN 978-0-7566-3826-9 (Hardback)
ISBN 978-0-7566-3827-6 (Paperback)

High resolution workflow by Media Development and Printing Ltd, UK.
Printed and bound by L-Rex, China.

Discover more at
www.dk.com

 **READERS**

READING 3 ALONE

My First Ballet Recital

Written by Amy Junor

Jamie looks forward to her ballet class. Every Thursday after school, her mom drops her at the dance studio and Jamie quickly changes into her pink ballet leotard.

She can't wait for class to start! Jamie sits cross-legged with the rest of her class, facing their teacher, Anna.

"I've got some great news for you," says Anna. "We are going to have a ballet recital. So you will get to dance on stage in front of all your family and friends."

Jamie is really excited! Imagine, dancing on stage for the first time in a beautiful costume with everyone watching!

"So," continues Anna, "You are all going to make up your own special dance. Think about what you can use in your dance that we learned in class."

Anna smiles. "But there's more good news."

"Tell us! Tell us!" begs Coco, one of Jamie's best friends in the class.

"Well, today, we have some very special guests coming in. But I'm not going to let them in until you've all done your warm-ups and stretches properly."

Jamie has always dreamt of performing on stage with her family and friends watching her, and in just a few weeks, her dream will come true!

Before Anna has a chance to ask them to, the students stretch their legs out in front of them and point and flex their toes.

"We need to warm up properly before we start so that we don't hurt ourselves when we're dancing," Anna tells them.

"Imagine if I hurt my leg and couldn't dance in the recital!" gasped Jamie.

"Exactly!" says Anna.

Jamie finds it hard to concentrate. She wants to know who their special guests are.

Pointing feet
All dancers practice pointing and flexing their feet and toes. This is a good way to both stretch and strengthen the muscles in the feet at the same time.

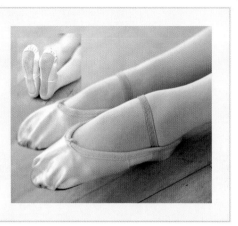

Jamie tries to sneak a peek at the door to see if she can see anyone.

"Jamie! Eyes straight ahead!" scolds Anna, smiling. "Now walk your fingers down to your toes and stretch."

Jamie and Coco try to do what Anna says without looking at the door!

Jamie turns her head and whispers to Coco, "Who do you think the guests are?"

Coco looks at Jamie. "I don't know. Maybe it's a ballerina!"

Anna sees them whispering. "Now we will warm up our neck muscles—although

Coco looks up, pretending to see an imaginary spider.

Jamie and Coco
seem to be doing
that already!"
Anna jokes.

"Sorry, Anna,"
they say.

The students
cross their legs
again and play
the spider game.
They look right up
at the ceiling stretching their necks
back, then pretend to watch a spider
slowly lower itself to the floor until
their necks are stretched forward.

It's time for the next exercise.
Everyone sits up tall, presses the soles
of their feet together and pushes their
knees down gently. Jamie tries to keep
looking straight ahead!

Anna gets them to stand up. It's really important to work on standing correctly. All ballerinas have great posture so that they can dance gracefully. Having bad posture will make some ballet moves more difficult and might even cause an injury!

Jamie takes one more look at the door and Anna catches her.

"It's very important to look straight ahead when you're standing up tall," says Anna, as she walks over to Jamie. Anna makes sure that Jamie is holding her head up high and looking straight ahead. Coco tries not to smile because Jamie got caught peeking at the door.

Straight back

April is another one of Jamie's good friends in the class. She always stands really nicely, so Anna asks her to show everyone how not to stand by arching her back as much as she can. The bend in April's back is the shape of a banana so Anna calls it 'banana back'!

Banana back

"The best way to make sure you don't have banana back," says Anna, "is to watch yourself in the mirrors."

The dance studio has enormous mirrors all the way from the floor to the ceiling. Because the mirrors are on two sides of the room, the class can watch everything they do to make sure they are doing it properly.

The studio also has a beautiful piano. Music is an important part of any ballet performance. The class listen carefully to the piano music and

imagine how they would dance along to it. Is the music happy or sad? Fast or slow?

The last thing they have to do before the guests arrive is to practice the five basic ballet positions. Jamie feels like the warm-ups are taking forever! The class have only learned the first three positions. In a few years they will learn the harder last two. Practicing the positions to music helps Jamie to do them all in one slow and flowing movement. Many more difficult moves are based on these simple steps.

Jamie can do fifth postion with her arms but not with her feet.

14

Jamie concentrates on moving her arms and legs into the correct positions at the same time. There is so much to think about! As she practices over and over, Jamie wonders how she can use this in her performance.

First position

Second position

She holds her arms out in front of her and presses her heels together to do first position. Then she slides out her right foot and raises her arms above her head for second position. Jamie brings her left foot in front for third position and lowers one arm out in front of her.

Anna shows them how to do fourth and fifth position.

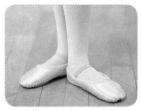

Third position

Fourth position

Fifth position

Finally, they are warmed up and it's time for the guests to arrive! Martin and Amy are two of the best students in the whole ballet school. They have come to show the class some harder moves that they will be able to do one day.

Demi plié

Jamie is so excited. She remembers watching Amy in a performance of *Swan Lake*. Amy wore a beautiful tutu and danced so gracefully that Jamie decided to become a ballerina that night.

At the barre
To hold the barre properly, Jamie and April stand a little distance away with both hands gently resting on the barre and their elbows slightly lower than their hands. Then they turn to the side and hold the barre with one hand.

The students do demi pliés holding onto the barre, then April shows them a demi plié without the barre. With her feet in first position, she bends her knees halfway.

"We're going to show you a grand plié," Amy says. Holding onto the barre, Martin and Amy stand with their feet in fifth position. They gently bend their knees all the way down, pause, and stand up again.

Jamie is sure that it's not as easy as they make it look! Anna asks Jamie to show their guests the dégagé steps she has been practicing. The class first learned how to do dégagé while holding onto the barre. Without the barre it's much harder not to wobble, but a great way to learn how to balance.

Jamie stands in first position and rests her hands on her shoulders to find her balance.

Jamie is nervous to be showing her favorite ballerina how she does this step! Her nerves make her wobble a bit, but she focuses on looking at a spot on the wall like Anna taught her.

Jamie slides her left foot to the side, careful to keep her toe pointed, then puts her heel down and stands up tall in second position, looking straight ahead. She points her right foot to the side and moves back into first position. The class claps.

Jamie is relieved that she did well and sits back down next to Coco.

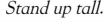

Point your left foot.   *Stand up tall.*   *Point your right foot.*

"Would you like
Martin to show you how
high he can leap?" Anna asks.

"Yes!" answers the class. Martin
walks to the edge of the dance studio.
He runs a few steps and then leaps into
the air. As he leaps again and again,

Martin makes it look easy
to glide gracefully across
the room.

"Why don't you try leaping
like Martin?" asks Anna.

Joe is one of Jamie's friends in class. Joe has always liked running and jumping. He runs across the studio and leaps into the air, keeping his arms and fingers outstretched. Looking straight ahead, Joe concentrates on where he is going to land.

He does so well that Anna asks him to show the class. Joe doesn't leap as high as Martin, but Martin has very strong leg muscles from years of ballet practice. Joe's muscles will be just as strong if he practices!

Joe has so much fun leaping that he decides to use leaps as part of his performance.

Joe loves the feeling of leaping through the air. Just for a second, it feels like he's flying!

Today everyone has been doing a lot of movements by themselves, but many ballets are performed in pairs.

Dancing with another person is called dancing *pas de deux*.

Martin and Amy often dance together. They can do things dancing *pas de deux* that they can't do dancing by themselves.

For example, when Amy stands on one leg, in a position called an arabesque, she can hold the position for much longer when Martin helps to hold her.

Martin has to be very strong to be able to lift Amy high in the air while she holds a position, and also to spin her around gracefully.

Jamie and her class won't learn to dance like this until they are 15 or 16 years old, but sometimes they do get to dance together. When Jamie and Joe danced together, they started to become really good friends.

Amy and Martin change into one of their favorite stage costumes to perform another dance for the class. Amy loves this beautiful tutu—and wearing a tiara!

Martin needs to be really strong so that he can lift Amy high in the air.

Révérence
At the end of their performance for the class, Amy and Martin each take a low bow to thank their audience for applauding them. This is called a *révérence* and is a polite way for dancers to say thank you at the end of a performance or a class.

They dance beautifully together. It is important when dancing *pas de deux* that the dancers are in time with each other and that all their arm positions and the shapes they make with their bodies match perfectly.

It takes a while for dancers to be able to dance together well like this. Amy and Martin have been dancing *pas de deux* for over a year now and their movements are in perfect time with each other.

While she is watching Amy dance, Jamie is fascinated by her special ballet shoes. When the dance is over, Amy shows Jamie her shoes, called pointe shoes.

Pointe shoes have a hard block in the toe so that ballerinas can dance on their toes. Amy's dance in pointe shoes is so graceful, that it reminds Jamie of a fairy princess. Suddenly she is inspired for her own dance for the recital.

Amy lets Jamie practice tying the ribbons on her shoes.

Jamie will create a fairy princess dance. She is really excited imagining herself twirling and leaping across the room in a beautiful fairy dress!

Amy lets Jamie hold her shiny shoes and she can feel the soft satin fabric on the outside and the hard block on the inside. Amy teaches the class how to tie the ribbons on pointe shoes properly.

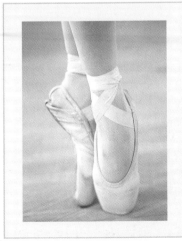

Tying ribbons
Ribbons on pointe shoes should be tied in a special way so that they don't get in the way of dancing. The ribbons must be crossed over at the front and wrapped around the ankle. Then the ends are tied together in a knot and neatly tucked in.

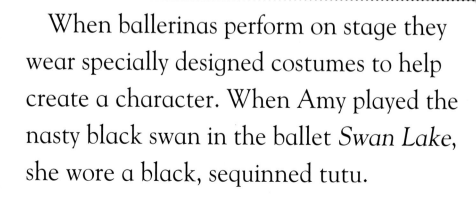

When ballerinas perform on stage they wear specially designed costumes to help create a character. When Amy played the nasty black swan in the ballet *Swan Lake*, she wore a black, sequinned tutu.

The girls in the class touch the soft
fabric and sparkling sequins. They all agree
that this is the most beautiful tutu they
have ever seen—even though it was worn
by an evil character!

At the end of today's class, it is time for Martin and Amy to leave. Everyone is sad to see them go! When a performance finishes on stage, the dancers are often given flowers to show how much an audience appreciated the concert.

Now that the performance is over, Martin and Amy show everyone how they walk out on stage to collect their flowers. Martin bows and Amy curtsies. They both do it perfectly.

Jamie presents them with a bouquet of pink and white flowers nearly as big as herself!

Then she thanks their special guests for showing them so many wonderful things.

Amy accepts the flowers from the class with a curtsey.

The next week, Jamie is so excited about class that she is the first person there!

"Today, we are going to learn about storytelling and expressions," says Anna. Many ballets tell stories, so ballet dancers have to tell a story without using words. Emotions have to be clear so that the audience can understand what is happening.

The class practice lots of expressions, such as happy, sad, scared, and angry. They express these emotions with actions. April stomps to show she is angry. Jamie dances with light movements to appear happy.

Happy

Angry

Sad

Shy

Another really important part of performing is creating a character. To help create a character, Anna teaches them about make-up.

Make-up for the stage must be exaggerated so that the audience can still see it, even though they sit quite far away.

Painting your face is a great way to become a different person, an animal or anything you want!

April puts on a headband with white,

pointy ears and scrunches up her nose.

"I'm going to be a cat!" she laughs.

Jamie loves helping April become a cat.

Jamie draws whiskers on April's cheeks and colors her nose so that it looks just like a cat's nose.

Then Jamie looks through the make-up box to find make-up that she imagines a fairy princess would wear. She pats face powder on her face with a cotton puff and makes her lips sparkle with shiny, pink lip gloss—just like a fairy princess!

Jamie tries a few foundations in different colors to find the right one for her.

Dressing up is so much fun! No character is complete without a costume.

Joe tries on a hat and waistcoat from the dress-up box and instantly becomes a street urchin.

Alex wears a long, brown leotard. When he adds some brown ears that he finds in the dress-up box, he immediately looks just like a fox!

April tries to find something to complete her cat outfit. She finds a white leotard to match her headband.

Now that Alex looks like a fox, he practices walking like a fox too!

Tutu

Jamie pulls everything out of the dress-up box, looking for something a beautiful fairy princess would wear. Finally, at the bottom of the box, she finds a big, white tutu that is perfect for her dance!

Now that April looks like a cat, she has to move like one. She walks with quiet, stealthy steps and imagines that she is ready to pounce! At the end of the class, they all take their costumes home so that they can practice dancing in their costumes before their performances.

Today is the last class before the recital.
Jamie is excited and a little bit nervous!
They practice making up dances to music.

*April feels elegant
and glamorous
wearing the tutu.*

The piano music is light and swirly, so everyone spins and twirls around the room. Jamie imagines she's a fairy princess and moves with light, airy steps.

April dances and spins with happy, light steps.

April puts on the white tutu and makes up a new dance. Wearing the tutu makes April feel very different to when she was dressed as a cat so her dance is very different too. Making up a dance like this is called improvisation.

Demi pointe
To dance lightly across the room, April dances on the balls of her feet. This is called dancing demi pointe. Young ballet dancers practice dancing demi pointe so one day they can dance on pointe.

The boys pretend that they are jumping over crocodiles.

Joe and Alex have become really great friends.

The music changes. It is now energetic and fast. Joe and Alex love being able to run around. They practice the jumps and leaps they have learned, trying to find out who can jump the highest and leap the furthest. Both of the boys want to use lots of different jumps in their performance and the music is perfect for them.

They practice fast jumps, slow jumps, long jumps, short jumps, and making different shapes in the air.

At the end of the class, Joe and Alex run and jump out the door. The next time the students are all together will be the recital! Jamie waves an excited goodbye to her friends Coco and April.

Finally, the day of Jamie's performance has arrived. She is really nervous and excited that she is about to be on stage for the first time! Her family and friends have all come to watch her debut.

Jamie keeps her head high as she spins... *and leaps across the stage...* *finishing her dance gracefully.*

Jamie has been practicing for weeks now and knows her dance really well. Her hands tremble as she puts on her beautiful white tutu and paints on her stage make-up. Once she is in costume, Jamie looks exactly like a fairy princess and is ready to dance! She twirls around the room and leaps through the air with light, graceful fairy steps. It feels like magic to be dancing in front of everyone and seeing them smile as they watch her perform. In just a few moments, Jamie forgets she is on stage and is completely absorbed in her dance.

When Jamie's dance is finished, everyone in the audience claps.

Jamie can see her parents sitting at the back of the room. They smile at her proudly, which makes her feel even happier. Jamie's family walk up to her on stage and give her a lovely big bunch of flowers as a present for being brave enough to dance in front of everyone.

It reminds Jamie of when she gave flowers to Amy and makes her feel special.

| *Jamie practices a curtsey.* | *She holds the edges of her skirt...* | *...points her toe and bends her legs.* |

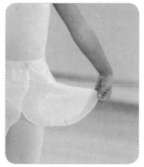
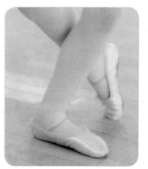

Jamie uses all the tips she learned from Amy to curtsey perfectly.

Jamie loves hearing everybody clapping because they enjoyed her dance so much. She feels herself blush and curtseys one more time. Afterwards, Jamie can't stop feeling very excited!

This is the best day of her life!

Jamie can't wait to perform in front of everyone again!

When the performance is over, Jamie doesn't want to take off her fairy princess dress and April doesn't want to stop being a cat! They are all still really excited as they change back into their class clothes and sit cross-legged on the floor. Everybody claps for each other because they did so well.

It was so much fun to perform on stage and to watch each other. The class can't wait until their next recital. They want to start practicing for it right away!

Although it was a lot of hard work for a few minutes on stage, they all think that every second was worth it.

Glossary

A

Arabesque
arab-ESK
A position where you stand on one leg with the other stretched out behind you.

B

Barre
bar
A wooden rail attached to the wall of the ballet studio to help you balance while you practice your exercises.

C

Costume
An outfit that helps to create a character.

D

Dégagé
day-gar-SHAY
When you point your foot to the side, front or back in preparation for moving.

Demi plié
dem-EE plee-AY
A half-knee bend.

Demi pointe
dem-EE pointe
When you stand on the balls of your feet.

G

Grand plié
gron plee-AY
A full knee bend.

L

Leotard
The stretchy clothes worn by dancers.

P

Pas de deux
pah der DUH
Two people dancing together.

Plié
plee-AY
Bending your knees.

Posture
The way you stand or sit.

Pointe shoes
Ballet shoes with ribbons and hard blocks at the toes worn by female dancers when their feet are strong enough after several years of training.

R

Révérence
rev-er-ONS
The curtsey or bow at the end of a class or performance.

S

Studio
The room where you learn to dance.

T

Tutu
too-too
A dance costume with a frilly net skirt.

Index